DOGS SET XI

Doberman Pinschers

Kristin Petrie

ABDO Publishing Company

visit us at
www.abdopublishing.com

Published by ABDO Publishing Company, PO Box 398166, Minneapolis, MN 55439.

Printed in the United States of America, North Mankato, Minnesota.
102013
012014

Cover Photo: Alamy
Interior Photos: Alamy pp. 7, 17; AP Images p. 9; iStockphoto pp. 11, 12–13, 13, 15, 19, 21; Thinkstock p. 5

Editors: Tamara L. Britton, Megan M. Gunderson, Bridget O'Brien
Art Direction: Neil Klinepier

Library of Congress Cataloging-in-Publication Data

Petrie, Kristin, 1970-
Doberman pinschers / Kristin Petrie.
pages cm. -- (Dogs)
Includes index.
ISBN 978-1-62403-102-1
1. Doberman pinscher--Juvenile literature. I. Title.
SF429.D6P48 2014
636.73'6--dc23

2013025490

Contents

The Dog Family

Watchdogs, hunting dogs, and show dogs. Big dogs, skinny dogs, and mini dogs! As you can see, dogs come in many shapes and sizes. But despite these differences, they are all members of the family **Canidae**.

All these dogs are descendants of another Canidae family member, the gray wolf. Early humans noticed the wolf's excellent hunting skills. So, they trained wolf pups for use as hunting dogs.

In time, humans began **breeding** dogs for different jobs. Some breeds continued as hunting dogs. Others were guard dogs. One of these working dogs is the Doberman pinscher.

The Doberman pinscher

Doberman Pinschers

The Doberman pinscher originated in Germany in the late 1800s. There, tax collector Karl Louis Dobermann wanted a medium-sized dog to protect him while he worked.

Dobermann experimented with several **breeds**. These included the Rottweiler, black and tan terrier, and German pinscher. His work resulted in the Doberman pinscher.

By the early 1900s the breed's popularity had spread across Europe. When **World War I** began, thousands of Dobermans served as military dogs. Many dedicated breeders sent their dogs to other parts of the world to save the breed. In **World War II**, the Doberman was the official U.S. Marine Corps War Dog.

The **American Kennel Club (AKC)** recognized the Doberman pinscher in 1908. In 1921, the Doberman Pinscher Club of America was founded. Today, the Doberman is the AKC's twelfth most popular **breed**.

In Europe, the breed is known as the Dobermann. There, many countries forbid cropping a pet dog's ears and tail.

What They're Like

Doberman pinschers are in the **AKC**'s working group. They are intelligent dogs. They are also muscular, energetic, and fearless.

The **breed**'s guardian instincts make Dobermans popular for military and police work. These qualities also make the Doberman a good guide dog breed. They can be trained to call for help at the onset of **seizures**. Others can assist disabled people in their homes, or work as therapy dogs.

Doberman pinschers can also be loving family members. This social breed prefers to be indoors. It is curious and wants to be included in family activities. Many Dobermans are so affectionate they are called "Velcro dogs." They stick right to you!

Karma is a search and rescue dog. She looks for people who are lost.

But be careful! This dominant **breed** may attempt to run the household. However, adequate attention, training, and **socialization** will result in a devoted and loyal family companion.

Coat and Color

The Doberman pinscher's coat is short and coarse. It lies close to the body, giving the **breed** a sleek appearance. Oil from the skin gives the coat a healthy shine.

The coat can be black, red, blue, or fawn. All Dobermans have well-defined, rust-colored markings. These appear above each eye, and on the **muzzle**, throat, and chest. They also mark the lower legs and paws, and the area below the tail.

One might think the short, smooth coat requires no grooming. However, Dobermans do **shed**. Weekly brushing will remove old hair and skin, distribute skin oils, and improve circulation.

Black is the most common coat color, followed by red. Blue and fawn coats are rare.

Size

The Doberman pinscher has a medium-sized body. Males stand 26 to 28 inches (66 to 71 cm) tall. Females are 24 to 26 inches (61 to 66 cm) in height.

The muscular body is dense and heavy. Males weigh 70 to 88 pounds (32 to 40 kg) on average. But, they can weigh more than 100 pounds (45 kg)! Females generally weigh 66 to 80 pounds (30 to 36 kg).

The Doberman's sleek neck supports a wedge-shaped head. Its almond-shaped eyes are dark in color. Its **muzzle** tapers into the strong, full jaw.

Some Doberman pinschers have **cropped** ears. They stand erect and pointed. Natural ears fold over in a manner similar to other hounds.

Natural ears and tail

The Doberman's back is short and straight while the chest is full and broad. The tail is typically **cropped** to the second joint. Natural tails are similar in length to other dogs of similar size. The Doberman's powerful legs stand straight and tall on compact paws.

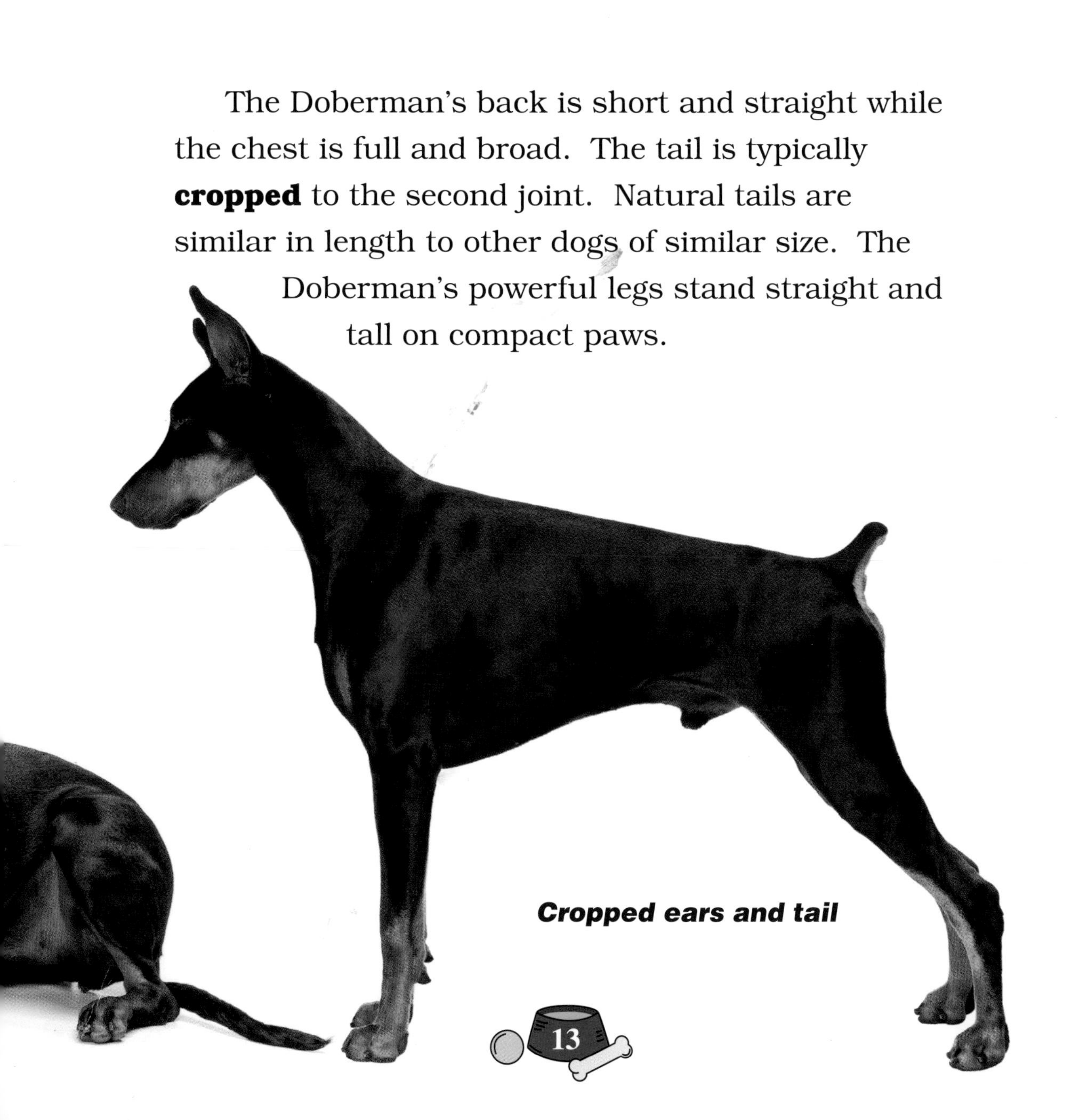

Cropped ears and tail

Care

The Doberman pinscher is generally a healthy dog. However, like all dogs, the Doberman needs a good veterinarian. The vet can provide health exams and **vaccines**. He or she can also **spay** or **neuter** your dog.

At home, you should brush your Doberman's teeth every day. This will help avoid tooth decay and gum disease. Dobermans also need their nails trimmed. A good time to do this is when grooming the dog's coat. It is important to begin these tasks early in a puppy's life. That way, the dog will become used to them.

Another important part of the Doberman's care is exercise. These active dogs need more exercise than many other **breeds**. Make time to exercise your dog every day.

A veterinarian can watch for health problems such as blood and spine problems, and heart disease.

Feeding

All dogs need a healthy diet. This is especially true for the active Doberman pinscher. Protein, carbohydrates, fats, vitamins, and minerals are important. They provide for growth, energy, and a healthy immune system.

A quality dog food will supply needed **nutrients**. It comes in moist, semimoist, and dry versions. Try different flavored and textured food to find one your dog likes.

Young Doberman pinschers need plenty of food to fuel their growth. Puppies need four feedings per day until about 12 weeks of age. At three to six months old, puppies can eat three times a day. After this, two feedings a day are sufficient until adulthood. Adult dogs can eat once each day.

An occasional treat will make a Doberman happy!

Active dogs that get plenty of exercise can easily maintain their weight. If your Doberman gains weight, ask your veterinarian for a feeding plan. And don't forget! Fresh water must be available every day for these vibrant dogs.

Things They Need

What does your Doberman pinscher need? You may be surprised by one of the essential pieces of equipment. Toys! Yes, the big, fearless Doberman pinscher loves toys. Balls, tug ropes, and bones help meet the Doberman's need for interaction and activity.

What else does a Doberman need? Exercise! Dobermans need outdoor areas to roam and run freely. This may be a large fenced yard, field, or dog park. A sturdy collar and leash are needed for long, frequent walks. Identification tags will be helpful if your energetic Doberman becomes lost.

A dog crate is good for travel as well as for training. The crate provides a safe and calm space

for the Doberman. Some dogs sleep in their crate. Others need a dog bed. Sturdy food and water dishes and treats are also necessary.

An active Doberman is mentally and physically fit.

PUPPIES

Doberman pinscher females are **pregnant** for about 63 days. After this time, a **litter** of 6 to 10 puppies arrives. The puppies are born blind and deaf. They are completely dependent on their mother for 10 to 14 days.

The puppies stay close to mom for food and care for eight or more weeks. **Weaning** happens naturally during this time as puppies replace mother's milk with solid foods. This time with mom and littermates is essential for the Doberman's physical and emotional health.

When the puppies are 12 weeks old, they are ready to go to a loving home. Is a Doberman the right dog for your family? If so, look for a reputable **breeder**. If the breeder believes you and a Doberman would be a good fit, look for an alert,

active, and curious puppy. Its coat should be shiny and its eyes clear.

Doberman pinschers need strong leadership. Start training and **socializing** your puppy right away. The bold, intelligent Doberman is happiest with clear rules and boundaries. A well-trained Doberman will be a loyal family companion for about 13 years.

Puppy school is a good early training option. There, puppies learn basic commands and socialize with other people and dogs.

Glossary

American Kennel Club (AKC) - an organization that studies and promotes interest in purebred dogs.

breed - a group of animals sharing the same ancestors and appearance. A breeder is a person who raises animals. Raising animals is often called breeding them.

Canidae (KAN-uh-dee) - the scientific Latin name for the dog family. Members of this family are called canids. They include wolves, jackals, foxes, coyotes, and domestic dogs.

crop - to cut off the upper or outer part of something.

litter - all of the puppies born at one time to a mother dog.

muzzle - an animal's nose and jaws.

neuter (NOO-tuhr) - to remove a male animal's reproductive glands.

nutrient - a substance found in food and used in the body. It promotes growth, maintenance, and repair.

pregnant - having one or more babies growing within the body.

seizure (SEE-zhuhr) - an episode of disturbed brain function that causes changes in attention and behavior.

shed - to cast off hair, feathers, skin, or other coverings or parts by a natural process.

socialize - to adapt an animal to behaving properly around people or other animals in various settings.

spay - to remove a female animal's reproductive organs.

vaccine (vak-SEEN) - a shot given to prevent illness or disease.

wean - to accustom an animal to eating food other than its mother's milk.

World War I - from 1914 to 1918, fought in Europe.

World War II - from 1939 to 1945, fought in Europe, Asia, and Africa.

Web Sites

To learn more about Doberman pinschers, visit ABDO Publishing Company online. Web sites about Doberman pinschers are featured on our Book Links page. These links are routinely monitored and updated to provide the most current information available.

www.abdopublishing.com

Index